Anatman, Pumpkin Seed, Algorithm

LOSS PEQUEÑO GLAZIER is a native of Tejano culture, from the southernmost tip of bilingual south Texas, and works and creates in that fertile multilingual overlap between innovative poetry and the languages of computer programming. He grew up in Texas, Japan, England, and California, and has lived and traveled extensively in the Caribbean, Central and Latin America, Europe, the Middle East, and South Asia. He is the author of the award-winning *Digital Poetics: The Making of E-Poetries* (University of Alabama Press, 2002), several other books of poetry, and numerous digital poetry projects, including ground-breaking works such as "Io Sono At Swoons," "The Clinamen," "White-Faced Bromeliads on 20 Hectares," "Mouseover," and "Viz Études." His work has been shown at various museums and galleries, including the Guggenheim Museum, New York, and he has lectured and performed throughout the U.S. and in Latin America, the Caribbean, and Europe. He is a poet, professor of Media Study, a Poetics Program Core Faculty member, and Director of the Electronic Poetry Center (http://epc.buffalo.edu), the world's most extensive Web-based digital poetry resource, at the State University of New York, Buffalo. He is organizer of E-Poetry: An International Digital Poetry Festival, the first and one of the most celebrated digital poetry series in the field. Glazier's selected digital projects and other work are available at his EPC author page (http://epc.buffalo.edu/authors/glazier).

Anatman, Pumpkin Seed, Algorithm

LOSS PEQUEÑO GLAZIER

SALT

PUBLISHED BY SALT PUBLISHING
PO Box 937, Great Wilbraham, Cambridge PDO CB1 5JX United Kingdom
PO Box 202, Applecross, Western Australia 6153

First published 2003

Printed and bound in the United Kingdom by Lightning Source

Typeset in Swift 9.5 / 13

ISBN 1 84471 001 7 paperback

SP

1 3 5 7 9 8 6 4 2

Para Francis, mi ser

Contents

Acknowledgments

Some of these poems have appeared, in variant versions, in the magazines *Basta, Combo, Compound Eye, Crayon, Eco-Poetics, The Experioddicist, Kiosk, The Little Magazine, Lower Limit Speech, Mirage #4/Period(ical), New American Writing, Poetic Briefs, Poetry New York, Rampike* (Canada), *R/I/F/T, Salt, Situation, Small Press Traffic Newsletter, Sub-Voicive Poetry* (UK), *Tads, Talisman, 33 Review,* and *Tinfish.* They have appeared on the LINEbreak program and in the chapbooks *The Parts* (Meow Press), *Leaving Loss Glazier* (Paisán Press), and *White-Faced Bromeliads on 20 Hectares, An Iteration* (Spontaneous Generation). "O : La Habana" was originally created for a Lit City limited edition broadside. Special thanks is expressed to the editors of these publications.

I. The Parts

The Apex

That the "rub" was translucent

get it, of fifty-two cards each

line begins a new number as such

not static – in what you said,

I can't remember the exact words,

but there an *apex* and facts of

conversion? Needed to fall up

on this notion, a mag, monotone

definite eruptions of insular

"song" (as a first degree) thus

white space of days   between

missives and the quote about thru

cells, "something abseils". That

small? List of forty indicators

in a wave (inappropriately shelved)

velocities adhere here's the </p>

Herr Foley's "date with loss" (send

me the quote, can you?) of some time

past – the link – here perhaps elec-

tronic – sense of the musty rolling

hills (who would have thought such

in 'there's no there there' – but of

course, where there's smoke there's

one about to cough) – with whom were

you entwined in that enjambed port-

cullis – back room reading – musty

fram'd buildings stave, stoa, saturate

blossoms never drop 'there' – heavy

names dominates dimlight prolonged

breathing, evening 'there' – a rose

garden flung or clinging to a gulley

roses parted there red spondee culls

in middus of the h'llocks, as houses,

les musty bloossoms cling thorn-strung

to cracked, emand iss asphalt paths

cordoning way 2 the particular bench.

Initials left 'there'? Hour's late.

Even such, present interrupts – was

recalcitrant – not to abruptly defer its

bench marks (start subsequent coleice)

to come home crushed. Days Latvian

should ave ore's linger. Dia. A lect.

A tres, e.g., as it has three strings.

Or slush'd cess of sheep misplaced

sevets reawaken lodge to night (com-

pound confusion of subsequent day)

somehow imminent as inaugural fall

storm furtive sweeps across flat

escarpment blusters Niagara frontier.

Most importantly, influential, or sign

holds 'place' or segment in piece

its dull approach shreds idea of

talk, said its *frame*, inside ere.

The Com'ns

As with the hundreds of files
per dye formulation (but see
it's not the *number* as much as

the "patching" – weave as the
ply resulting in branches seem to
make it find. Sheer exhaustion!

a part of sense of what does pry
apart. Until on the "line" other
issue of this. It's as if the alert

where its brambles from Fort
here and see with you who wrote
'not about bits, bytes, bells or whistles'

paper . . . where the rouse . . . and to
words characteristically spread
familiar even while reading that

If you possess strong verbal skills
you are 85% more likely
to achieve your career goals

        (day in
D-town . . . your words on screen
marked as people's next-in-order.
An assay, missed approach

stow saturnine slope
a selvage or sauvage
romance wets orange blossoms

crisp russet grooves
body maximized by its moves
specific and enduring

a soul
but
no-soul

incrementally, a precise
mode or method per
abridgement.

ABCDE

In thE Experiment. 'What
is this "anGel of incidence"
haT trick that permutation
of it? For example, screEn

stRands in its own address, to wit
there must not be intervening *sLip*
of paper.' (Paper as the peel –
old standby for burlEsque.)

*Take word processors. They haven't increased
production. People don't write more letters they just
revise them more times. And spell checkers have NOT
increased clarity but the number of times Say, a
wrong word is used but spilled right*

it and send it. You can even
compose as you wait for the other
winDow jones to load. AnY Bits

are better than misplaced cUes.
If only lone momentary wRiting
perhaps to thE Point?

NoT aUtomatic. You of it
is translent. The veneer and
varnish of "producT" apes

the baSe seem permanent.
Sans horns but perfectly
post-Modem in congestIon.

How I Was Attila in a Past Life

Losing its words. Take some aegis or exit point where alpha
types disperse. The family grows old and leaves without you.
There was some hook to holdings how the etzels regenerated.
The 'rod and cones' of it. As it was penned, the bull waiting to
bolt forward but the human cannot wait for sunrise. Hence
dismemberment makes a myth of words salving a permuted
path. Veneering through https, Dogtowns backed up on reels
of glossy Roman polymer. Whose words you see *everywhere*.
Hums: restrict yourself to writing on mainframe. Spaces are
collapsed by some protocols but it is not confused by
underscores. (Though your sometimes use of parens makes
cursor leap in half-tangoes, pistachio, and Abba riffs.) Was it
worth a single screen? Can it apprehend the reference applets?
Simultaneously you are free to receive invasions from across
the continent. It's the local disruptions that bludgeon Bleda.
Does the ghostly quality that these marks are not *impressions*
but literal *absences* in a blue background replicate a mimeo
master? Ride ghost-framed. Its evasion demands only half a
Western Empire as dowry. There is urgency since flukes occur
and if the contraction cuts, its image evaporates. This only
exists within the buffer unless you write to disk. No record of
his motives for typeovers into Gaul remain.

On the Occasion of his Return to Civility

who also our bard being Zeit

reading Time und in the stacks.

No mere 'meaning' but reader

who knows the response of

'to book it'! Philosopher who

also boldly goes forth where

no cablegram has gone before

but unto the Net, who knows

its broad-bend palmetto pattern

what Campbell's might find in such

nodals. Time being lost

because that long http will not

band any more than sight

Five Pieces for Sound File

> Let poetry return to its first purpose, the oral
> message. Let there be a law against writing
> poetry. It should be spoken then recorded.
>
> Kerouac

Is the formal space or foregrounding
(public : space bars ticks)
of the arrangement of words
as for presentation;
seen only on vs. the British
heaviness of "lark"
in the U.S. we tend not
to name our words
crisp white page. The self-consciousness
of it, or premeditated aspect *exiting*
via Estonia.
Baltic coast spudgies; that is the mistake
of 'soul' for 'coast.' Old Soviet maps
altered to discourage boats traversing
Baudrillard's "continuous present".

Now that sounds can be edited
on hedgerow. Cam culls, at least out there:
Who are the real Amblyopians?
along riverside, figures predict presence
singing a full-throated path through young pastures
afternoon sex in a room above the pub
and along the footpath an inn where sitting
self-medicating in batches heavy resin
clocks, under weather, and girasol
resound as though there only for us.

What erasable mountains are those
where we supped and eye turned to
the only inn at the end of the lane
alert for signs of prey
in the Thames estuary
pine and pico paled; *thrushes*
feeding on the gerund
graphic of gear pene-
trating plot.

Without humor, the words are doing what? I
wanted to hear elevated language or be in
a circle of floating capital, ESP
in a gentlemanly accent
in which da blur lost 'er audience.
She is drawing loss on her notebook
"his first poem a story" then font
fiction between present and feature;
hatch faction of veered angles, certain
of the low end of plantain in transcript

on the verge – that constituent contact
ends – though I'm no diner King –
it meant so much and again will
break his I – does it falter?
Like the note passed in the row ahead
this terrane of books is the whole of language
how we navigate only – piecemeal.

Proposition (Octave)

In the chaos it wasn't Blake
surprised its cavity among
shards undo shreds of moon
predicate of tern's erratic
night-latent methaqualone
bred amid wild cactus spurs
under skin swell and redden
form its chore brisk tipped
nigh emporia classed et see
la ciudad de Alicante tiene
almond-flavored horchatas a
frantic San Juan celebration
abandoned station where oars
beat wet plum slick on split
periphery of ebony lippd bay
I didn't want to say that not
at least bend of rhizome tick
it's not leaving to represent
any radical read "approach"

~

unsound cross-stitched a piece
its improvisation of afternoon
arc of campo del sur y catedral
tea, C. epicurean calamari veil
pulling wefts & rounding after
spin-offs across its crumbling
wall a (carte postale) crushed
concatenations oblivious unto
Moorish blue lager submerged
lacquered spill of entourages

effort's emblem at least par-
layed to earthy contours wrest
(immaculate in plastic seal)
of delicacy: "not just *Spanish*
olives but olives from Seville"

⮾

precision, sounds suggest
lacing needle strokes beck
vers impediment – ask not
what yr caesura can do for
you but what you can do for

⮾

stricken in shell find a macro
motherboard's inculpable misse
"intoned a metronymic stroke":
wanton, weary-eyed, leverd fin
de sickle slants and implodes
history [sic] of meter, art, & c.
maritiming et equipage of canal
parlay aphasiac noon knew no
intrepid lips so in transitu
calm as saguaro-chiseled "send"
slatch released incarnate rung
does it evoke Unamuno, gallery,
lisp London angle, hard to pin-
point save irregularly recessed
from the busy street. A dormer
room weaving dusty hallway lest
sower a clutter of corroded pip.
Not until you are naked bitter cold

in the public shower do you read:
'Insert coin for hot water'.

~

got shallow "ey" of this
thou write thereof gives
rise a chalk spur I elides
when you voiced 1969 did
you think that's 17 year
to their (18 if so, there
are at least eight vols.
to be writ, i.e., reply!

~

routinely incensed car cast
here also a mural rampart of
Palacio de Justicia AKA such
portraits of Machado, Lorca,
& Hernández who died there
projects train horn seaport
plagiarized clings vine com-
missural mulls rift-wood harbor
across defined icons sourly
invoked I did marvel file Menu *is*
Meant to Pyramid word's site

~

encephalitic axiom lies con-
nives the broker planning "the
revenge of the octet" in which
main players reveal the abject "it
was full of rackets, balls and other

objects" predicament mimed "quick re-
search" pulling out snake-skin laptops
spinning ten gallon cranked A:\ drives
there's not tha' much to inculcate
beyond innate indexed abstract stacks
an esplanade, opening to circular
peak or focal point of its park.
A made object taken as a whole
that bench, and up the road a
store, with at least memory for
data. Data do's and data
don'ts. Then the bench again
as with the line, people who
are pronouned routine pass,
and if you decomposed there it
would only be *yr* aberration.
user would read the paradigm
might be shimmy they say one
rock plus one is one rock, si?

∼

this mise they say to interpret
title as a proposition (hence
"The") it is unrest that follows
in phone calls ring to Iberia
West Acton or an Upper West Side
the whole enchildada's subsequent
attempt – as if defining "quid"
that argument patently specious
undertake bronco fiber motion
burrs presage ointment lodged
rust breaks pliant facts emerge
that radix sum to labyrinthine
graphical plies of prehensile web

Parsings – from *E*

> To the winds shall be thrown
>
> words being wind or web

SUSAN HOWE

The writing method. Some would find it hard to distinguish from NAVIGATION. Or as features:

* precariousness of the LINEAR
* special interests
* suffixes
* the role of the Internet
* list movement
* hyperbole
* the laundry
* circumnavigation
* retraction

An extension would be formed. Necessary to see idolatries in a fashion. Start with this, open that; could keep opening indefinitely. Of course suspension of closure may be the attraction. On the other hand, what about EXTENDING practicalities of what might be written in making possible its emanation and constitution as ARRAYS of what – we're not going to try to mount that poor old tired hocked "information" here, are we? About as useful as *About* in the drop-down list box and it tells you diddly squat, like who wrote the program, when what you want is to know what it does, if anything.

∼

Like mapping software which recognizes neither the starting point nor the terminus and is thus unable to draw its 22.html.

If you can't find any hot keys in these frames then you just have to back up until you come to some kind of fork that allows you to choose a path different from that which you previously chose.

I'm putting in the html indicator at top though I have no idea what it does. Looks organized anyway.

∼

A form of disclosure.

[IMAGE]

∼

I believe the calendar read "Camilla unzips the file". At least the pattern on the camisole would lead one to such an ardent desire.

∼

You feel it's not even *work*. The point being that it's not an established genre or form of writing. Not a forum, nor an essay on modernism. Hey, think *Essay and Literature General Index* is going to pick up this racket? Or you can leave completely. Said it's not the point. You fell asleep or got working (cf. a crime to concentrate) then overheard people got married, had babies in the meantime, etc. Now that's a link. (Wink.)

A man alone in a modest room. You find his glasses, the impression of his body on the bed, and think, he had form, he aged, his artifacts. Content to be a sanguine body in a place in time. He was alone but his Bodhisattva sang.

~

Weekends sunburnt, sequoias stunt scrub stammering
turquoise ballad ripped antipodal with absolute erectile
abandon the sharp curves, imbroglio, and thrusts
mounting the flesh pink ridge.

Everyone screaming they're going to be killed by this Anáhuac – what was the point of the speed and spin-outs dangling on the jagged curves? Some possession or fait accompli that co-anchored not only bodies moving like evaporation to the sun but indexed intense chaotic hyperbole of passion. Beaujolais nouveau. Bowdacious nivel. Would lead spring-fed to satiate question. Articulate. Meniscus. Sediment, that's your fate.

~

Now it's with them. Black Sea's Italiante vistas. Hallucinogen of semi-submerged villa. Diving naked into sea, as easily as if the horizon were your mind. Who weren't there but were at the CRUX of the anxious escape, now aged, see-through though not slipping. Venetian blinds. The same coaster and there's a handrail to grasp as the room rides up the incline then tumbles in exact photo-replication of what was there, after parking on narrow side streets, past Turkish stalls & cheap prizes.

Eating by scarfing what people left on plates. Aubergine intoxicant. Inexorable entourage of minaret – sea-blue oxygenated ash. "Maybe she's his soul mate." Maybe not.

≈

Say there's always a way back. Click or clique, it's all the same.

≈

I heard it was because they wanted to confuse their enigmas.

The Parts

Anesthetic of snow, earlier, whether
in repeated stay or what hustles those
days – white's eclipse – as in "too

much white showed in his eyes"
could make an event the long
parabolic through white to connect

about an idea. But here it is,
convert wave to author, concatenations
of technical parts; its scatter deflects the work

printing it out is only parts of
it, sections somewhere framed
and amenable to being scribbled on

so that perhaps it's a matter
of clippings you assemble
scrap book fashion strings

of form dispersed by light. Ambling tile,
pocket phoneme, montane cloud forest,
the Cuban parakeet, Zapata wren and Zapata rail.

Hair mussed, tossed back, similar to the case
of "mode" as the first Internet flicker known
world wide: "woman in car laughs".

Triad's sweet penumbral decor:
inbred talk, animated faces, charm
postaxial cosmetic engorged to scale.

At such a distance pausing or side-
stepping, ancient sabal palm, streaming
water towards a zydeco Venus, gumbo, andouille –

as the saying goes, "First, you make a roux".
Then there are subjects that cling
fan palm to any sense of "making" pigment

so intense that holes oboe in living
canvas. The double-edged incongrous ex-
orbitance with which squall surrounds song –

wet writing wouldn't want to. Matter
of the "word". Cubano sandwich,
chat for a bit, if you'd thought more

you might have gotten to the
point that *Poetry does not
gain from mummified speech.*

"Ellipsis" is incision point and
conversely prolapsed. Whether there's
part for want – strong pull-time

parses. Kin to "living" in a period
of adapted measure. There should only
be one book, writings weave through that.

II. Semilla de Calabaza (Pumpkin Seed)

White-Faced Bromeliads on 20 Hectares (An Iteration)

1.

Ambience or collocation. "Colonia" as in that sense of "colonial".
Do you mind if I slip into something more comfortable? Like what?
your public underscore html. A guidebook called *How to Write
Whining Resumes*. HTML as the world's dominant language. As in,
contact glazier at ak-soo. Well, I bet it has something to do with
Nahuatl. Po cenotes. Act of Tejanismo. "You speak so many
bloody languages yet you never want to talk." Metal models of now-
room mansion. Aztec flowers. Can't recall one thing I ate in quetzal.

2.

It's an inter-text. Its inherent collapse of serial syntax. It's not what Icon going in a barrel over Saigon falls. We'll have a couple of flurries for breakfast. Files containing text loss investigators. Not an Ivy League egg. "For every man in my life I have a new scent." "What confusing and mazing things sentences are." I con, I can, I cheat icons. As a shortcut, I speak through the ventriloquist. "He did not have a clear impression of water cress." I will now toss gloss of Los Angeles, Los Alamos, as in One-Eyed Buttercups.

3.

One small cup on the (World) Wide Verb. 24 inches in 24 glaciers.
"We're the Glazier family, we eat what we want, when we want."
Spanish, the only language better than UNIX – keep an eye out for it!
His signature señor right-eyebrow-arch under the volcano, my
cactus studded slopes. Guanacaste, the unglamorous national tree.
World's most famous mangrove cadence. Isabot, iceboat, sabot,
isobar. A number, an umber, adumbration. "Oiseländ" for example
coffee fields. Narrow seats and coffee-can sides of rattling bus.

4.

Nicoya. Nica. Tica. Medellin. How to transfer the lines so line
endings grab a break. San José calles, three chapulines roving to
attack stragglers, coconut hillocks yucca bottle-brushed shampoo
the taped and tattered bills to pass to tourists. 700 colones or $2.60.
A sudden downpour (that's why they call it a rain forest!) I have
yet to eat in Costa Rica. The modest national clay-colored robin.
Take a dollar, fold it lengthwise, then in half for multi-colored
bottlebrush. Caribeño, bananas. *fronds*. Ah, ¡Es la Fortuna!

5.

Finding a pumpkin *seed* in your vocabulary. A dead tree becomes
a bromeliad altar. Policía Rural. Brahmin cattle. Los Angeles,
Costa Rica's fresh furrows against smoky ridge. Banana chips on
the bus. Una casada, comida típica lava gushing glowing twilight
plumes & sputters. Before sunset, bathing in a river heated by
lava's flow. "Bromeliads" con bromas. Empanadas, the emphasis
on "filling". "Bocas" meaning "for the mouth" as language forms
fills the mouth, tongues of tropical light – pura vida, compita.

6.

Renamed "Fortuna" ("Luck") when it was the only town left after
buzz-dived by 6 a.m. hummingbirds volcano with shroud six years
ago and never left, leggotts, open waisted, fresh-washed canary
scent. The eggs with salt, black-sugared coffee, how it papayas
upon tree stalks in front of undulating cane fields. The sap can burn
your lips savia blanca de la papaya. Ginger plantations 3 or 4 days
for potent licor de piña. El Flechazo, hundreds of sunlight-slurping
iguanas form a vivid green canopy above the trees. Mi hijo lagartijo.

7.

Agua sapo, "toad water", sweet licor served cold with ginger &
lemon, particular to Caribbean coast heat. La burla y la ironía. I
would like to show you the way from La Fortuna to Los Chiles.
Tico Fruit Finca Cinco. Banana plantations. Despacio. 52 Cabo
Blanco. Those are paper trees. Howler, Spider, & White-faced.
Tree frog. Naranjas tropicales. Chickens, tin shack, white-humped
cows, egrets. Moon-crater pot holes. Green-back heron, Anhinga
(snake bird). Wood storks, verdigris river – flurry of long nosed-bat.

8.

A Jesus Christ lizard on the basilica. Bats take off. Rio Frio's
green egret black bill yellow feet. Blue-bodied Amazon kingfisher.
Red flash of social flycatcher's yellow breast. Three camens eye.
Toucan at last! Fingers arched – international symbol for toucan.
Picnic under ceba. Yaxche, sacred to Mayans for equilibrium.
Zanate o clarinero grande. Black and rich sound como clarinete.
Mirlo Pardo. Yiguirre. Bosque Lluvioso. *Sloth* glazier. Sleeping
hummingbird doesn't wake – even to camera flash in volcanic night.

Xochimilco

A gap of some 8,000 years appears in the cumulative
archeological record between the prehistoric carved
coyote head from Tequixquiac and the beginning of
a recoverable sequence of words. Even talking about
it becomes confusing. Códice Chimalpopoca, fish
carved in mother-of-pearl and greenstone. The
capulli and capultin. Stone rapture of rattlesnakes.
Granite grasshopper. Did the shells foretell the sea,
the crocodiles a terrestrial level, and Xiuhtecuhtli
and Tlaloc the celestial striation? Voila que c'était
là. The Chihuahua rebels ambushing the federal
convoy, stripping the dead soldiers, then sending
the empty uniforms back to Don Porfirio with
Orozco's "Ahí te van las hojas; mándame más
tamales". ("Here are the corn husks to fill; send me
more tamale filling"). A Porfiriato of prosodic
extremes. *Offering* 58. 1. *Sawfish.* 2. *Turtle remains.* 3.
Conch shell. 4. *Human skull.* 5. *Alabaster dart.* 6.
Alabaster deer head. 7. *Little shells.* Aztecs driven out of
Chapultepec in 1319; Aztec chief and daughter
executed. Coxcox (Pheasant), ruler of Culhuacán,
then giving Aztecs a barren gully in which to settle.
There was great amusement at the Aztecs, butt of
Coxcox's joke, since the gully was crawling with
rattlesnakes. But it turned out the Aztecs were
rattlesnake-meat gourmets and they cleaned out
the gully with gastronomic zest! HuitSILO say for
example for a nuclear weapon. A tienda de raya. Or
Díaz Ordaz's dastardly conduct in Tlatelolco's Plaza
de las Tres Culturas. Náhuatl *is* Méxicano.
Hummingbird resting on palms. 20 rockers, known
in México as "chavos banda", along with four police,
were hurt in the melee which began when police
tried to stop a spontaneous sonnet in the main
plaza of the suburb of Nezahualcóyotl (suburb

named for "the poet"). "And we saw the aqueduct of Chapultepec, which brought pure water into the city, and the drawbridges which allowed water from the lagoon to go from one side of the causeway to the other." The Ángel de la Independencia, fifty meters above cars trumpeting round its traffic circle. Golden angel on stone column, round-terraced base holding ashes of Allende, Hidalgo, and other heroes. Oaxaca morena walks by as chamomile breeze is absolutely careless in wispy shirttails and long dark letters. Born in the small villages of Jalisco and Guadalajara, mariachi music is abundant with strings – violins, guitarrones, vihuelas and guitars mark a moon-like, full rhythm section. The underneath of the monument worked with aquatic motifs, as though the etchings floated in lime – or a liminal state – just at the edge of figures at Cacaxtla, the Classic Zapotec or Maya, Café Tacuba, the rock group by the same name. On top of that sensual, rich sound are the singing trumpets and clairvoyance. Landscape like coastal California curves, ocean, and pungent fragrance of weeds, plants baked with hot air on the winding road from Pochutla to the airport at Huatulco. Wind's totalizing hot blasts of dry herbs and stunning pitched vistas of sea. High rolling, speed, the bargain you struck. San Agustín, Chachacual, Cacaluta, Maguey, Órgano, Santa Cruz, Chahué, Tangolunda, Conejos. *Bahías de Huatulco*, 2/18/97, 4 P.M. You haven't seen an airport like this, eh, con palapa y refrescos. Straight necks of bottles glimmer in restaurant overlooking Casablanca tarmac of tourists and one-liners. The distinctions they perceived between the gachupines and themselves were increasingly galling to the criollos. Although

no more than 10 percent of the former were
legitimate hidalgos, the peninsulares persisted in
their pretentious manner. Shortly after this
interview the Mexican literati went to work. The
Yucatecan sociologist, a positivist but not a
Porfirista, published an outstanding prose volume
entitled *Problemas de Posadas (Poseidon's Tostadas)*
shortly before lunching on yuca. This was just
before the teen-age Madero was sent from Coahuila
to Paris and then to Berkeley for proper grooming. A
Pequeñismo? Don't forget that in a book on *Mexican*
history the chapter on my birth state is usually
titled "The Loss of Texas". (Though I prefer, "The
Lhasa of Texas".) Sister metropolis of Tenochtitlán,
Tlatelolco, Aztec stairs leading to sinking Catholic
foundation. Built directly upon remains of the great
pyramid climbed by Cortés. "We were amazed at the
multitude of canoes in that great lake, some laden
with foodstuffs, others with different kinds of wares
and merchandise." (Would you call it twisted that
"Cortés" means "courteous"?) The Spanish brigands
were conquering a city larger than any city in Spain!
A recumbent figure of chacmool bearing a Tlaloc
rain god mask. On his chest a cuauhxicalli, a lava
stone vessel for sacrificial human hearts. He wears a
pendant with an archaistic motif to refer to things
of antiquity in general. Alternately called Venice of
the Americas or Paris of the pre-Columbian. In
Oaxaca, researching for weeks the exact room
where D.H. Lawrence stayed in the Hotel Francia,
tracing Lawrence's steps through hallways and
cavernous hotel courtyards. Reenacting exact
passages from *Lawrence in Oaxaca*. (They even keep a
copy of the Spanish translation behind the hotel
desk.) Then, at night on the Day of the Dead, woken

by his frail ghost clattering pallid through the room. I didn't believe it. And never having seen that image of him, hunted down a book I had not previously known. It was his exact image! In Zipolite, people amble au natural on wind-swept sand, an elevated wind, surf thunder. A photo of the items on your mantle carried and placed by your hotel bedside. *Offering 52. Painted turtle, a clay coyote or maybe tepesquintle, a dog raised as food. Monte Albán pottery shards, images of Che and Karl, obsidian Tlaloc.* One of the tropes has to do with México, not Plymouth Rock, as the historical center of "American" culture. (Plymouth being that original hard rock cachet.) That is "American" more broadly seen and "culture" if you include what occurred before 1865 or so, i.e., before the U.S. industrial revolution. Near Xochipala, in Guerrero, have been found a number of clay statuettes dating from about 1,300 BCE, modeled with a sureness of hand and tortas tantalizing back lanes of Coyoacán. Persimmon Casa de la Malinche, intertwined roads, sun plastered on plaza, coyote sculpture crowns mango palace facade. No matter how lacking in education and culture, they considered themselves superior. The press pointed out that that the egotistical Lombardo had used the word *I* ("yo") sixty-four times in his farewell address and took the occasion to dub him "the Yo-yo Champion". The little mute hairless dogs they so loved to eat. Yappy but yummy. To think that someone could become stranded on this stretch of sand. Offering to work for board doing laundry rather than face the Mexican road. The German in the photo on the boat at Mazunte with Pacific spray in a doleful, dolphin-piqued breeze. Holding the rudder so the two barefooted fisherman could wrestle the tuna to the deck. As if her simile could ever wrinkle. ¿Cómo no?, wash and guero. "Among us some soldiers who had been in different parts of the world, in Constantinople, in Rome, or in other places in Italy, said that they had never seen a marketplace so large, so well ordered, so well controlled, with such harmony and with so many people, as this one." 97% of all Spanish nouns ending in the letters L, O, N, E, or R, are masculine. Does that fact tell you anything about male asocial tendencies? Mariachis, the point being they stroll *to you* to make music. "*Yo quiero Taco Bell?*" – *No, yo quiero civil rights.* The meaning of "Zócalo", a pedestal, i.e., making public is to place into view. The center square of a pueblo (also meaning "people") or a place where texts are made prominent to the public "I". (See the pedestal in the letter "I"?) Primetime news of TV Azteca, one of México's two major networks, with its recumbent gods that, animated, rise from the sleep-ridged volcanoes. From the Tlaloc side of the twin pyramid perhaps? The tlatoani was the conduit of order, the very figure keeping the upperworld and the underworld in their appropriate positions. Parakeet's bath and play perico nipping against the tanned smile's sway. Bare in short summer dress. Leaning towards the perico clearly. The first meaning of Náhuatlatoa being "to speak clearly" that is, to speak Náhuatl *is* to speak clearly. The Aztecs later earned their freedom by coming back with eight thousand bloody ears cut from slain Xochimilcas in the service of Coxcox. Coxcox was obliged to give them his daughter to become their goddess. Imagine his horror when, attending a banquet in his honor, the entertainment included a dancer dressed in the skin of his flayed daughter. The point being that "ILOVEYOU" can be said in so many ways. Better terms are perhaps Méxicano and Castellano, O Señor de Texcoco. Mi loco. Though the languages are similar, the influence of indigenous forms upon the latter give it not only an opposing ideological base but a divergent lexical grounding. Surprised by the hallucinations, mi pequeño amor? It's not ayahuasca, it's ayuthink. With a ~ on top of the n of course!

Mezcla

Where are the hills? I ask. The pip en el
habla. Soplan de cuatro partes del mundo.
Significant and, in the blazing sun, el palacio
terrenal al cual llaman Tlalocan – perched on
expanse of sage. In Mixteco, sobre las piedras
("lost with coyotes"). It can be seen in the
eyes. "The old man says when he met me I
was infested with disease. It was only
tuberculosis!" Only the Quebradas open to
winds on partitioned land. So plan day tress
party dale moon doe. San Antonio always
being México's capital outside México. The
Flores Magón brothers, Arriaga, *Regeneración*
offices, and Madero's base. Thoughts are
covered: el zapote, la guayaba, el ciruelo, el
aguacate y la chirimoya. The sabbath, the guy
yapper, the cruel yo-yo, the hour cutter, the
shitty lawyer. Outdoors and, "It's hard to pin
down why it's different." (Is the fee seal
parachute tar cone all feeler a bathrobe pour
quinine different?) Lines defer geometry
branching raggedly around engraved tufts of
puckered rump. Calypso rose and carnation
pink is splayed its inflated pouch-like lip, no
doubt. Este curiosamente es mezclado, sus
idiomas, color lavanda, y también dogs in
back. And what about the aquifer? Would
wake Cristiana and frightened she might
scream. Still no choice but to venture where
the invalid matron is stretched, a raspy,
whispered plea. Después, sense of routine
digging in cupboards, the teabag must be
fifty years old, is torn and has bled a brown
stain. Ether's curiosity is muscle dough, sue
idiots, color lavender and temblor dogs in

back. These are rare to find since "tea" here usually means chamomile – then outside to smoke. Fervent green grass, "winter" corn, cracked concrete, dogs, los perros andan y allá, me siento that *its language sheds our corrugated skin.* Tin roosters crow ornately errable, brazen-feathered starlings busy hovels clothed in green mesquite, pecan arbors, the wet, low lying valley; barbacoa where years ago they gathered with corn, cerveza, and cabrito. Little changes – age chaparrals their faces, bodies bloated, names of streets follow fracturas de la corteza terrestre derived del latín "facienda," "cosa por hacer", yards cluttered, colored pennants listless above a stored boat offering shade for the dog's somnolent yawns. Culebra, Buena Vista, General McMullen. "Por qué eres dolorosa?" At the market when buying a tape they ask if you wish to test it to see if it works. Well, why not? Baptized at the Little Flower Shrine via Santa Teresita. Panorama of su cabecera, scribed in stagger plumes of passim light where near the Asadero Culebra a worker from Durango sings in shade "la alacrana que me mata es una hija de María" ("the she-scorpion that kills me is a daughter of María"). Loll a cranium chemist maddest toon as ether María. From the flap in which appears the figure of Estebanico, simply referred to as "the dark one" in historic accounts. Dice it, you know the story, one of the four survivors ("supervivientes" or "super-livings") of the expedition of Cow Head (Cabeza de Vaca), wandering from Florida to

Sinaloa. Eight languages learned in the passage; heat of immersion in the way ordinary cactus overfilling wedged precipice. La viejita always the last vestige of our first tongue. Block stains elevated. Lace cloth for the groans thrown into the grove; words that you pronounce as you put them into cracks etched over projecting squares of stone – quarter spine figure of the corn men with feathers, sweet wrinkles, and each woman with the cosmic rectangle anticipated by whatever god of the breeze. Enabling me to offer. As projections for roars of the tempest. The earthly palace called Tlalocan; by this wind it is called tlalocaiutl – it's not a furious wind for the predictions, for the groans, soil terraced in rocky tables. Pronunciation is impermeable. Crustacean. Concentrated tines. Crumbling into morphemes as you fumble into trilobite cracks. El rectángulo cósmico. They blow from the four parts of the mound. The palatial terrarium all squall yeoman Tlalocan. El huey tlatoani era el jefe máximo de los aztecas. Eh hooey heavy maximum deal oh's adz ticklers. Noah's vent furious parallels aquifers, loss ham-eaters chaos room. Mentira assumes facts not in evidence. Nasturtium: a moment of petaled recollection you can pop bright-orange to flower in your mouth. "These are curiously mixed, your languages": the collage as continuous prickly pear shadow lining cool sand with spine-covered, but edible, Bexar stems.

Ideographs, phonetic signs, and rebus writing.
Tomato, chocolate, avocado, coyote, and ocelot.
"México" meaning "in the valley of the moon".
Mole poblano as mole from Puebla. Poker faced
panegyrics. Civilizations progress from 1500 BC
to 1500 AD. Olmecs, Teotihuacan, Tula, and
Aztecs. (With Mayas active throughout.) En-
veloped again by the tropical turquoise sea of
maternal language. Saints want flutie. If less is
more then loss is Henry Moore. That's why all
the appendages of these poems are so bloated!
And why they sometimes stand out in a park in
the rain for days before they are viewed. As to a
gloss, "loss" is mired in some kind of rhyme
game. All the granite brought in from Brazil.
Whether from the white place of herons (Aztlán)
or the Seven Caves (Chicomoztoc), the apple
doesn't fall far from the poetry. Tlaxcala, "place
of maize cakes". Tlaloc glows. The Merced's
artificial mounds like ziggurats in México,
carvings which recall the reliefs of Shang
dynasty bronze or in Peru. 1996, Formation
processes of the archaeological. 1996, Zapotec
civilization : how urban society. 1996, Historic
Zuni architecture and society. 1996, Digging for
dollars : American archaeology. Others are of
youths dressed for the ballgame – a religious
ritual as well as a sport. Near Xochipala, in
Guerrero, have been found a number of clay
statuettes dating from about 1,300 BC, modeled
with a sureness of hand. For example, a poet is
un poeta while poetry is la poesía. Un poema
follows un poeta but la poética is poetics. Who'd
a thowtit? A sensitivity to three-dimensional
form and a liveliness which suggests an

established tradition. The figures from Xochipala
are the first works to be associated with the
Olmecs. Challenges to habit like remembering to
throw used paper in the basket and not drop it
in the bowl. Their formative influence on the
first civilizations in the Americas is what
Sumeria was to the ancient Near East. And
stanzas on stele stand to us all.

La Habana / Mar

00 MAR. Floating across days of reclining the
chair and visiting the back seat as Tejano
countryside rolls past. Will's smile. You try to
catch it on film but it's as clever as the breeze.
Now we've returned and residues cannot be
remaindered. "The clouds look like Antarctica and
the blue is the sea." Leave it then. Whack of big
slice of cheese pizza into a starving beet. Entire
industry producing stream of consumer tips for
those who want to find "beauty". Quiet, you watch
a whole planeload of ribald Germanic sentence
structures. Bring on the Anglos & Saxons too, why
don't you? In that conversation when papa says
"I'll bet voters in the USA wouldn't take what the
Mexicans do" I launch an eloquent rebuttal saying
"I'm not right about anything. Why should I
interfere with your cockney critique of pure
raisins?" Anyway, I can wait. Just ring the bell –
tocar el timbre, touch the stamp – or however it
translates. The timbre thing. Waiting, watching,
writing, worry-worting, oar leaping at limber
phantoms exuding the scent of attraction or even
a loss hum. Despair! Despair! And you, García
Lorca, what were you doing down by the window?
The cicada in your hand, "wounded by invisible
swords from the blue"? La rumba. "¡Yambambó,
yambambé!" Get up and run off the plane. Or yet,
the unrelenting refusal to give up on hoped-for
explosions of fruitopia, green, white, and red, the
chance to immerse oneself whole-bodied into
cascarones of fragrant nights. Erupting in
scintillations of pastel confetti. Is it contradictory
or emblematic that next to you chez Lufthansa
towers an enormous Germanic woman? More
giant than human. Covered with scars and rattling

du's and dienz. You are a midget in a mountain
chain or ballast for a bloat of flesh. Or could it be
that some touch a tint hovers outside of limits,
colors, hue-words don't matter; nor does music.
Aracely, in a building on Rio Sena, who books
passage to La Habana.

04 MAR. A post. In olden times that the minute
you hit the plane it would be a torrent of words,
worse n endz from edge. That was the deluge you
thought of as, wanting to post but out of time or
felling renuncia, the obvious how to read as a
possible contribution. It's inevitable such torqued
dynamics will shift from the inside & out. "Positive
redundancy." How you bracket text blockquote but
also perhaps again time to consider how to read
backslash-blockquote. Not realizing what dramatic
dusk would drape or that these days we even have
magazines on the topic of *living* so far removed are
walkways, horticulture, handicraft. We've been
through almost every argument about this: that
print is portable, that it's tactile, that it's
somehow more substantial. The kind of burly man
who comments loudly when you take a long time
in the airplane bathroom. You can fill out personal
inventories, set goals, and see if you get there. It
warms outside. Night blossoms filet the air.
Suddenly, ecoutrements like limes are bountiful,
pungent, & sparkle in crisp carbonated water.
Lengthening hours. People of varying ethnicities
begin to predominate. Days before, out of the blue,
he was thinking whether to have fish or chicken.
"They'll think these pants are baggy but tomorrow
I'll put on my suit."

11 MAR. A TV sports announcer with bad teeth. A
salsa line of small islands, coral visible beneath
lambent sea. "When you get your period you
become señorita; when you marry, señora".
Cerulean of the Caribbean palpable from palapa
sky. A couple always has some form of consensus –
this is helpful during time zone changes. Plane
descends into musk of music. Instead of ads by the
road there is "Siempre Rebeldes", "Socialismo o
Muerte", and signs arguing knowledge, belief in
Fidel, Che, la lucha. Within minutes of arrival a
schoolteacher hands me a copy of Marti's "Los
Zapaticos de Rosa" insisting that I read it on the
spot there in the arcade. Entre rosas y camelias.
"Nice shoes." Making fun of Mexican accents.
Night ambles through spots such as Café Paris,
Hotel Ambos Mundos, La Mina, La Torre de Marfíl.
The sonero, person who leads a son with a nasal,
more high-pitched tone. Concerts occur outdoors.
Bar Parrillada, a Marc Antony slash shish kebab
joint jab salsa-stepping chef. They serve beer in the
camera store. No negative to that! Adalberto, who
fits my square shoes.

13 MAR. A man pretends to be a taxista so he can
demand money for carrying my suitcase out to a
real taxi. Moré. Brocheta. 20' high ceilings and
cigars. Cerveza Hatuey Clara. It has become
impossible to scribe. Color and movement on
Havana shell. A cold snap puts temperatures in the
60s. My brocheta served with sliced tomato,
cucumber, and pineapple. Apaldor, romantic
crooner who is chileno. Showing the dueño my
cross accents pen. Cabaret Nacional, Hotel
Inglaterra. Stores have nothing in them. Whole

families on a single bicycle, wall paintings of Che, TV Telerebelde. Lluvia de Oro. Radio Revolución always playing through perforations in thick walls. Milanes perhaps? Mi amor mi ma mi ma mutu aw tu ma. "Mi Tierra" in rehearsal. Los Van Van. You don't just ring, you hollar. Ry Cooder's coveted cover of "Chan Chan". Jineteras beg you to buy them cookies or mothers wish to exchange Che coins for any medicine you can spare. Luxurious views of the luminous sea, wheelbarrows of pumpkin, pumpkins in heaps, half-pumpkins, seeds blazing in sunlight. En cada barrio revolución. Socialismo o muerte. Oh you are licenciado. Crazed sister. Hay que tener bomba. Musicians moving together chez chan chan.

16 MAR. Box lunches for the beach. Bar Monserrate closest to Capitolio. NG La Banda de la salsa buena. Jesús Bello good CD. "The state owns everything". A slab of pork on a bed of rice and some beans in a cardstock box. Also try the chicharrones. Café de Paris's 24 hour police surveillance. Calle de Obispo. Bodegón, "La Lluvia de Oro", state owned restaurants, a grand cigar at the beach. Cuban parrot nest, Fernandina's flicker and the world's smallest bird, the Cuban bee hummingbird. Music everywhere. "But all I have is five dollars." "Very well then but, ¡No tienes vergüenza! Tu eres un hombre malo". No one has a match. Sometimes they won't sell you fries if there aren't enough potatoes. Bought a Che shirt for him. How much they charge tourists for the Museum of the Revolution. (You think that's expensive? Try marrying a Cubana!) Roosters, radios blasting, lines of laundry suture the interior

courtyard. No toilet seats or toilet paper. (The Cuban who on his first visit to the U.S. was taken to the Galleria Mall – he asked, astonished, "Is this a museum to capitalism?") Flies abound. Beef uncommon. The girls have to work. Grilled potato, pineapple, tomatoes, pork. Pan-sized pizzas for a quarter. Mama pinga. Mama bollo. Rey Luis. Casa de Música, the acclaimed music store, sparsely shelved but with some selection. La Rampa. The seat falling back with panic as you rush to leave. El flamboyan en nuestras costas. "¡Eso!"

ON YOUR MARX. "She is tropical, a Caribbean breeze, Cuban sol." The radiant birds exist in cages in two's – parakeets, lovebirds, and sulfur-crested cockatoos. The corner for birds, amor. Half-shell fountain, miniature orange trees form walkways, immensely pleasing to the self sense even as there are sones o salsa in waiting rooms. An effusively tiled Sevilla. Socialist radio of the Revolución. Standing still here one page six days letter. That sap of desolation when one can't communicate and at such a distance pausing or side-stepping from the accelerated pair of spiral frogs streaming waterward towards a Venus surrounded by citrus leaves, lovers, y café. If not paradoxical then a crime, the luxury with which one surrounds song sandwich Cubano writing wouldn't want to matter. You must make it to the Museo of the Revolución by three. There is some English spoken but in general there is not. What this might contribute to any conversation with mist wafting coldly in a patio away from the street bustle, a person seemingly wanting to walk and chat but at the end offering cigars, rum, other pleasures.

When a pair for example is broken up to go with separate men. (They will allow you to photograph their aura as long as they can cover their faces.) Carrying an average monthly income in your shirt pocket, though I still can't possibly afford a proper hotel. At 50 speedball cents a day it doesn't take much but the weight of its ballast is often quite audible. Ironically, the only place time has slowed enough to reflect.

18 MAR. IN CHE'S A WAY. Three days equally pages. Coin-sized hummingbird inches beak medalling luces blancas, pink, good to have a blanket again, green enchiladas, a walk in the clairvoyance of a clear De Efe night (Ver claro: Sol.) Verb. Verbena en amino. México, D.F., miércoles 18 de marzo de 1998. Reading materials. From La Habana in a plane with no first class. Labyrinthine corridors of La Habana Vieja. Medieval curving routes through crumbling facades punctuated with buildings now rots with rubble, having imploded, garbage fill lots. No me engañas hombre engañar i.e. give daño with people streaming skin colors a blaze of fabrics roast pork kebob or broiled chicken quarters. Cooking on a camp stove in a closet. Cuban coffee. Fabrica Partagás or Plaza de la Revolución. Music everywhere, rehearsals in rented ruins. Che coins salas del Che salsa Che murals the most famous being the building in the plaza and the trova "Hasta Siempre" by Carlos Puebla. (Surprised, when you meet one of Che's sons, by his rebellious manner. Later realizing that nothing could be more in character!) An avg. American has more in a suitcase than an avg. Cuban has in his home, refrigerator not included,

of course. The revered José Martí. Guantanameras
Ydarmis e Yelaine. "Chan chan" i.e. something
onomatopoetic. "Mi tierra" in rehearsal. Not about
memory but about the stone crumbling in
towering courtyard. A cockroach the size of a '59
Buick: it's almost manslaughter to kill it! Passing
hours within 20 foot ceilings, grand armoire,
mirror, headboard about to collide, Titanic-
fashion, with rum reasons & orchid iceberg of
sleep. It doesn't matter where you are. Suddenly, a
man might feel an arm inside his. The idea is to
have a refresco or cerveza, chat for a bit, a bite to
eat. It might involve a trip to a disco in Vedado or a
taxi ride for ice cream. Luxuries so rare. Physical
contact occurs at times. Appearing in public
momentarily acquainted, lips occasionally
touching, arms kept interlocked.

VIVA ZAPATA. Four folds or folio. Foils the
imagination doesn't some text upside down and
other parallel. Paz en español. Recently published
image of state mountains succumbing to cloud
smoke puffs. Sounds like the clacking of a for-hire
typewriter operator in the Oaxaca market.
Inundation's memory when the shiny word
"supermercado" was spoken. Lying on a grassy hill
as a child in Ciudad Juarez waiting for mother to
return from the multi-story open-air market stalls.
Perhaps that's why it feels so natural to voyage to
sound aromas the furrows of chaotic energy. Two
Rolls Royce Allison turbofan engines. Embraer,
pronounced like "Embray air". Combray flair.
Jordan air. Dijon must tardy be. "Life vest" spelled
as one word cutting across the Gulf of México's
four-hour flight. Saying to me, you should see La

Rampa at 8:30 "a point about which little has been written". What is physical contact in relation to the island's paper-translucent flesh of sun? Lucent technologies. Lupine fractals. Fracasos. What fetish fissure blessed stance upon la calle starved for articles of clothing or a night on the town. Willing to act almost for a packet of cookies, a carbonated refreshment, for some line of amelioration. It's all unfair. I am only a passerby reflected in a dislodged window pane. My words are little. Return flight near empty. Quick to call you borracho in the blazing hibiscus of the courtyard, the sun shrinking shade in the morning, hip cocked forward saying, "You should see it when spring arrives. It will be three days now, the 21st." How many newspapers can you read? The addiction spelled C-N-N. "What did I do wrong? Why doesn't he want to marry me?" the landlady is asked. Should one feel guilt over breakfast? Makes fruit somehow revolting. Quite complicated how high art gets high. Art consumption scourge continuing to the present from its 19th century antecedents: tuberculosis, scurvy, slavery, syphilis. No towels in the bathroom. To flush, you must dump water into the bowl with a bucket. If your timing is wrong, the ordure sloshes on your feet. "Once there were 8 small rats here but now they are gone. I don't know how, since the cat is also gone."

O : La Habana

Rooster's   courtyard   cramped   street
seller   of   poetry   **pamphlet.**
   La   Lluvia   de   O r o's   wood
   Alejo   Carpentier's   Volkswagen   bug
     (Tour   coffee   **harbor**
Converted   upstairs   studios   i. e.,   *barbacoas,*
     i n   s u m m e r   hea t .
   Lunch   peregrinations   salsa   rickshaw)
Where   inside   is   ah,   outside .   Statue   of
Jesus   atop   the   **hill.**   All   light   streaks .   and   cool
                 breeze
              o ver   wate r
         ship   departs
         (Yes,   I   do   see.)
     El   Cuarto   de   **Tula**   (Candela)
     dance   the   street   *freely*
High   antique   ceiling,   20   *feet of*   *filtered*   *light*
   aged   aromatic   lace.   In   a   *d r e a m* ,   an
         imminent   loved   one
              o   o
arrives ;   o   o
         familiar   o
         taste   o
           from   o
           inside   o
         her   o
       mouth   o
           o
     She   is   fragrant,   olive,   a   lion
     :   as   the   *oh*   in   (boca)
   out   to   medieval   *smoke ,*   Spanish   tower ,
         w e t   pavement   harbo r
     pas sages   twist   o paque   into
labyrinthine   opulent   caress.

III. Leaving Loss Glazier

The language you are breathing becomes the language you think. Take for example in UNIX (and UNIX is the wellspring from which the World Wide Web was drawn) to "grep" or "chmod," things done daily, possibly hundreds of times a day. When you grep ("global/regular expression/print") a given target, you search across files for instances of a string of characters, a word. To chmod ("change mode") is to use a numeric code to grant, in an augenblick, permission to read, write, and/or execute a given file to yourself, your community, and your world. These are not mere metaphors but new procedures for writing. How could it be simpler? Why don't we all think in UNIX? If we do, these ideas are a file: I am chmoding this file for all of you to have read, write, and execute permission – and please grep what you need from this!

Digital Poetics

Windows 95
For C.B.

> The primary building which divides
> come to Mayapán O how is known
> as "The Castle" or "Pyramid of
> Kukulcán". Anchoring albondigas
> loss investigators affirm that is lunz
> reminiscence, dale, O Chichén Itzá,
> others do not stand all accordion tall
> exacerbation.

I guess that's what all computers will look like, a leading
sentence and a pad that allows you to slide the triangulation
toward Perseus or whatever constellation supports such a 32-
bit encounter. The letter then – inside a box at the bottom of
the screen – describes itself as being "as easy as changing
channels on your television set". (*Obviously they think the most
logical pointing device a remote, not a mouse. This says a lot!*) But of
course we wouldn't want it to work out the way it did with
beta tapes, which were actually a superior technology. The
point being that the market favors the superior marketing,
not the superior product. "El Castillo" de Mayapán, un
acertijo, that it oscillated or was an "opus". Oh say can you see
this chronic it's not youapan it's myapan. Itsa well pooped
colonial medial conundrum designing restaurant chains. Best
to consolidate them, evacuate your bowels of farinaceous
structures of capitalism & put nail polish on quarters for the
juke box. (I stayed home today simply for the pleasure of the
housewife as Mayapán is clearer still from an origin of its own
instruction & if undergarments from Cambray as pans occults
the base of yage bury some lizard head of serpent spuming
foam a culmination cloud scales north castle of Chichén.)
10.0441 as the aesthetics of programming: "In a sense code
resembles classical poetry. The requirements of meter (poetry)
and syntax (code) pose both limitations and challenges for the
good poet/programmer to adhere to and overcome in the
process of writing a great poem/ program." The activity of
writing *is* to gawk, permission, and chmod all this into some

useable idiom – or hopefully even decent Latino syntax. The
presence of four escalators from the orient to four quartz
points drawn from blood cardinals whose cemented balls
structured the construction similar to the pious lizard head of
Chichén sugared a den of Mayapán tambourines press the
phrenal bliss of light's somber come equinox rhinoceros
springs atone. Passwords you mumble paying your money to
ride on someone's back across the rio. Rev. Mactlactionce-Calli,
Mactlactliome-Tecpatl, Tozoztontli Caxtolli per ducor, duceris,
ducitur . . . ducebar, ducebaris, ducebatur . . . Deuce o' spades,
do's and don'ts, do as I say, drag race, space out, let's deuce it
out ace, action figure, keep pace. "School" comes through Lat.
schola from Greek *schole*, "a place where leisure is enjoyed"; the
Run and Shut Down items have three periods after the item
name, and only a Help item is unadorned. These signposts are
used inconsistently to tell you what to expect. Keeping track of
laundry cleaning the quartz timepiece, a czar's Cro-Magnon
ointment, bull pens or flight, viz. you can't even count on a
good bass Stratocaster that indexes coal – foo on evolution of
any importance you urban columbines! How does it work? It
might freeze up on you and you lose every word or you might
discover syntax buried so deep your ancestors, even with their
dubious roots, provide no excuse. Deeply latent incremental
climb to sweeping sighs of dulcet mark-up. Fathom a lake of
sleeping children, a refrigerator in the barrio of shallow
graves, enter urbanity, your banality, basura, and original
dompe rules. La Virgen de Guadalupe's darkness suiting the
charro charro Mexicanos. The one of mixed race, of Indian
blood, the one for atravesados, those who cross cultures. Oh
my, a pan! Mebbe the natives will cook up some quaint tacos
light up under pyramids costs a notorious "Achin' Mule". If
now loss caved in and cenotes had grains, grackle, imprinted
parrots, parquetry, caramba, lost antiques, ardent inhabitants
of My, a pan, eat hay for your prostate's sake. Until the date no
see hath compromised that existence a relation in C-notes why

[59]

less structured pyramidal con games a center to this simply prehispanic, ciudad prehispánica. Across the tortilla curtain. In contrast, la Malinche is the archetypal victim; she who represents betrayal, the tolerance for foreign values, the conquerors. For example, someone who would argue the primary meaning of "tortilla" is "omelet" even though standing on the North American mainland. Or Shakespeare's colonial wench. Malinche also means translation. Like they say in the ads for the promised new world: on the minimum or maximum reserved space type the new disk in the Hard Disk box and type values (in kilobytes) in the Minimum or Maximum boxes. When finished, left-click OK. In order to optimize swap file performance, you might want to click your heels. We're a long way from flicking a Bic. Or having come a long way baby, where's my cigarette? No – hey – that Olivia Newton John depresses the workers realize in herapan sturgeons munch hippopotami – on a beach naked I suppose, bronzed and bulimic. The dénouement of the Maya, ideas that basted queue sure corroborated among fragments of dates ripe under fronds. Ever sit in a fast food restaurant and notice that there are so many ads on the windows for the latest movie theme tie-in that you can barely see outside? Windows offer slivers of context as a frame for commercials as content. This might be the ideal path for the Web, according to many developers, a place you catch glimpses of information as you view windows plastered with ads. Hey you could win big if you just peel the game piece off the side of your cup. Or register your software for the latest prize giveaways. You may have already won. If you have the right attitude towards directories you will never flail. After making your choice, left-click the Next button or pass go. Right-clicking a file produces a pop-up menu that varies by type. Artists tend to left-click while

Republicans tend to the right. If the period might've once been called "Error & After" it will now be known as "Eudora & after". Thorn and sing-shrub or Subject: I know I shall have awful DOS pains in the morning as a result of this.

The Figures

Perl or Java – go figure!

Nottes on desk – pages and further, that it becomes a
matter of *largesse* – per its Italianate origin, "solare"
for sun, "sodare" meaning "Go get us some sodas,
sonny". Add a twist of lime & do not index 'sodomy'
with aforementioned verbs. Don't get sore! Take its
'Wouldn't you rather have a villa than vanilla' and
add the image of flesh rising in middle-of-the-night
coruscation. The crepuscular image of the albino
giant's nude to Kyoto body clumping about the room.
White hairs on thighs racing like sea foam to an
iridescent cove. Her bulbous lower lip. Peering out
from the covers, it is strange and remarkable but
even more so: when Kobe gets into bed next to you –
you realize how warm and malleable the red tide is.
Sea salt sticks to your cells. You lick your lips and a
sick click fans you full sail. Like a gigantic bowl of
tapioca, sound oboe, or say your need to digress when
it comes time to clean your cannoli. Desire is the
enormity of the physical *otro* with whom you do not
have Texas. A syntax that accelerates as hard as
mescaline. Pause mid-meadow to retro recharge
cerebral tock. Atoms check for errant javas. Bend the
markup the way Dizzy did his trumpet! The camera
shifts to the raindrop effect to signature the look of
romantic love. Character set, on-the-fly code, a strictly
text editor bee-stings the upload. Check DOS figlets
landing an autogyro on a mango promenade. I adore
it! Where else can you have an atomic clock and the
phases of the moon right there in the title bar? In
script, 'of' is a set of headphones – time that accurate
is not for everyone! (Note how the single quotes cusp
the ears of 'of'?) The bomb bringing Odysseus to
monotone moon-blast architectonics. Vermouth

backed by lapidary palms. Times wingéd chariot, hours a passim, AKA can you Telemachus what time the computer clock will read in anno 2000? Check your iambic tick. If you want to be a muse of mine – then tally Homer! As my mother relates, "It only cost me a dime to get into this country". Or as I sometimes put it: "If this is the wave of the future then we all might want to buy some mousse."

Olé / Imbedded Object

> Mayakofsky said
> occupy their zonas rosas
> locomotive passing
> overhead on heavy
> trellis. See the mesa – i.e.,
> Take it to the bridge.

"Any given content any given person" stands against the
bayou on its "hunt for shells" – EMACS live and on stage!
Can you find its home page? At Perseus "Homeric"
as a qualifier in that what does it hold, haw, which vessel
is full now? Monday's new millennium can always wait!
So here are the important questions: What is OLE and
what does it do to a matador? I'll take milk in mine. As you
read on Mexica salt cans, when it's Tláloc, it pours.
And may Tlazoltéotl NOT follow you on your date. The
chafed hills rise, scrub succulents, precise blue above baked
passes. Acayucan to La Venta, venison at Monte Albán.
Tapped out for quick cash in Ixtapa, you call in your col-
lateral with Teotihuacán. A childhood clarinet. Some copper
coins. Comunque or communiqué moon communist. The
quarter noon is scratch & dent. Color & density cor-
rections for negligent negatives. Child emerging between
thighs of goddess like a bloated clay penis. Wherever you go,
there's an icon waiting for you. Most people will just wanna
thrust up their yams. These are behavioral versus statutory
conventions: zip drives, self-extracting files, translations, &
among their ambient pages the relative values of recent versus
"original" annotations. Voglio dire, if you can prove you
were thinking about this a long time ago, whammeee,
you're consistent sonny! Intercalated lettersine, CL, LC,
LG, and the final thematic frustration with it as letterism.
Decided to pull one of those cinematic formulae: man picks
city for final drawn out stanzas call it "Leaving Loss Glazier".
Ever think how your life would have been different if in 1989
you'd stuck to WordStar instead of switching to WordPerfect?

Their DLLs

Why do we not suspect them when they do an
anonymous login? Is it the silver screen? Is it
because you are *pretending* to be someone else? Is it
because a lot of people are watching? How is it
artistic to pretend to download a file you don't
need? Though these questions may seem reasonable
to the average applet importing partygoer, the
answer, my friend, is not to stonewall holes in the
desert. The 'That'll do, pig' as the waiter places the
adagio smack dab on the Mickey mantle piece. For
example your social security number is quite easily
intercepted from one node to the next or take
nosebleeds, the trouble with nosegays, and how the
rose knows no thing goes where their lever, wedge,
or inclined plane rows "off task". Frankly, what we
seek to convey is the value of metacognition. Not
'what I am doing' but 'what I am conceiving what I
am doing is doing.' It's all very simple. (You could
see his body language drop in an instant – though
they still made fun of his hair.) There you go. In
essence it's a tilt technology – more nihilistic more
Nietzschean anyway. It was another "P" thing –
error message – Perl of wisdom, piglet, or Javanese
amulet. Ah yes, about the gold cord. For more
information, see the section on platform specific
issues below the pen. Specifically, Eros can be
configured to remain a small icon on the system
tray (on the right side of the task bar). In addition to
context sensitive help there is the "what's this"
button in the title bar of dialog boxes: this cheery
tomato of a chip feature is also available by right-
clicking on any control. (Even your own lack of self-
control.) Though horticulture will not have the
3-dimensional, sculpted look familiar to many, it
does not calcify your Windows directories ("trash"

on the Mac) with a bunch of DLL's – with one
optional exception. Herbs. Herbaceous angora –
what? Who can live with them & who can live
without 'em? No chive. The "normal" use is to
create an icon for your own basal projections, as
unlikely as they might be in your startup folder (or
"group", if you're living in the past).

One Server, One Tablet, and a Diskless Sun

Idleness defined as a lack of keyboard
activity or waiting for crepuscular code at
the edges of a dram of shadow ram. Why
DAEMONS and why DEBUG? O María mía,
what could be evil or mischievous about
any of these applications – a daemon
being software that launches when called –
as in MAILER-DAEMON. And what do bugs
have to do with a machine not working?
Because in some early hacker's
imagination there were bugs crawling
around inside the CPU? What was he
thinking – or was it smoking? *And what
kind of bugs?* Lorca's mystical crickets?
H.D.'s butterflies? Though I think they
must – if the mind does have an eye – be
cockroaches fat, brightly lit, and mightily
glowing. Flying through the mind shaft to
assault any mental indiscretion. Perhaps a
relative of Burroughs introduced this
term? (Stick that in your machine and
add it up!) What vision of mainframe!
What robust modems! What processor
speed! (The word "mainframe" of course
so much in the outs that it can be
considered a true Freudian slip in
professional circles, to misspeak
mainframe for venerable UNIX SERVER, as
if there could be a MAIN frame to
distributed poetics!) For example,
dichtung und doppler stating which word
processor created which documents. It's
the same as knowing which grapes gassed
a specific grade of vine. Or videlicet: a
dictionary is strictly a discretionary

database that's lexical, languorous, and expressed with convincingly adamantine linearity. Dat a base, baby. Any Oracle experience? In Greek it's retsina. When you need to know, it's always time to write a technical paper. Because it's a journal file system. And the hours at Illiers ironing out a finite state machine. I mean, what if we *did* have an erotically charged world? How would this influence the weather map of the Net? Even the most innocuous guys would show up and need to have this image and know the words: *If I can read and write I can bear the strain.* Hungry wet grasping mouths circle beneath the rigid pole holding a set of stage lights. The check itself a serpent, made of thin ice, slides down the wet windshield glass. The sense of penetration is infinite. Seventeen stations of the cross, one server, and a diskless sun. With the appropriate C-bindings we can make use of an X-motif. *How* we are busy. What ways we'll make lists, whether on tablets, scrolls, or PDAs implanted in the crux of our most embarrassing events. If we lose data we don't want to take a chance of not recovering it, do we? That's the color of a multi-threaded compiler. As is argued: UNIX system administration has a *guild* because UNIX system administration is a *trade*. It requires the skill of the carpenter, guile of the metal-worker, the glazier in his glory. For one thing, there's no college degree for this profession: *you*

need to know how to do something! For
another, we look for people who
understand that computing is a lifestyle –
not a hobby or a job. That's always scraps
and bits. What was it called, "atub"? We
tried to decode that one for months until
we saw it was directory name shorthand
for "at U.B." Hackers! Who was it put a
bug up their ASCII? Or did they explain,
"It's just my ego speaking"? That is why
accuracy is achieved by reading a wide
variety of sources. Though the arousal can
be extreme, one must be moderate with
the sensation of sources. Information is
supple not erect. In other words, think
with your brain, not your hard drive.
We're the unacknowledged shaman in
the CPU cycle, the traces of pattern when
the screens refresh. We pick up the
pieces, bind your binary, put the boost in
your bouillabaisse. We're the salt in the
shaker & the spice in the puritan; we're
the lumens that crawl between the
windows the hesitations allow.

Direct Contact

I haven't heard a history of meaning for the
terms that calling the mechanics of poetry
tricks was punctuation. Scrolling retro
nomenclature did you say? It's not so much
an editor as design software? Then why does
the sound of flan mowers seem to redline you
from all three sides? And where are the
crows of yesteryear? The whole book has
vignettes laced with blank lines for latex
insertions. Ever consider that 'DOS' rhymes
with 'loss'? What about an operating system
built by Baba Ram Dass? (Such a system could
not allow multi-tasking since all tasks would
be one.) The computer user? This is narrative
itself: the replication of structures as you add
your own details. (Where it says "My other"
said, please insert "their real name".) If you
follow instructions, the coma that comes out
will be all your own! Call it "social text",
algorithmic excess, recalcitrant egress, or
metamorphosanarrative . . . say, there were
times I felt on the "outside" though I was in
the story line on day one. I so much prefer
the term "direct contact" or "one-to-one
correspondence", Bruce A. writes to back
channel which sounds . . . subversive or
gossipy or even *mechanical* I add, always
staging clear from it percussive or stet syrupy –
even the manual's in short sic supply. Which
might explain why Charles B. has no fear of
Windows 95. For me it seems the windows
work *against* each other – as if it occurs by
littoral miscegenation. Pay attention to what
winnows *between* the windows. Trying to
catch multiple leaks with a single sprocket.

The toads come out after it rains – but try to find one on demand! Paste it to another application to evade the canny *undo* that enables an errant dilettante to edit/modify graphic images and sound. I will look and see what might be up & yuppy by then! In studying what literary critics have said about its quality of pusillanimity. (To safeguard this, they suggest, make sure poems elevate consumption and its cohorts – individuality, superficial beauty, idealised attraction, the afterlife, & the viability of magnetic storage media.) This brought me to an adjunct misapprehension of the phrase I thought. The whole idea of representation is quite asynchronous with its *theoretical* position; its relevance to a text editor is socially apt even to the point of observing you do not actually *write* to a file. Think of "social text" in this manner. What you write to is a copy of the file which *exists only in the buffer*. Therefore what you write is not written until you choose to "save" it and interim changes you make are provisional. Imagine what that would do to speech. You could say the social is material – inside of it. You could then look at it and manipulate how it sounds. It will not be spoken until you "save" it or actually "send" it. Projection then among them an instance of extension of projection. Public would not exist until privates were swabbed then saved.

Del Rio

Strangeness of customs, that there are dwarfs in costumes,
mints on pillows, ease past fruit sellers & bought the old
hotel simply for other ways of standing. (Caucasian, light-
haired, & pert.) Sky globes bursting in paprika above
an "I want to look at you" immersion in a Guanabara cove,
candle-sellers, and household flocks. The nature of fluency
on the rooftop with the Boston view, sitting on the balcony
slats, or the late walk from 52 Park through the sultry Cams to
flesh a way to the opening lines. The object lesson, its youth
is in domestic language. Walk across the room in another
frame. The movement of a body from open rooftop
to kitchen floor. Open the way sighs are open or
gasps of anthologies in white or olive bottles on a
counter lags. Lentils, door frames, sight of linen, a
pearl. The church is a round face with moon ciphers
for an alter-. Summer legs. White-wash and pastels,
simplicity, suppleness, open limbs. Language is a
simple dress. That a backdrop or baía de such a port
in such a place would develop. Was it in the climate
or position of rocks? A facet? What causes an
appearance in such a position? Its half-light on a
strange city just after sun-up, its tangibility in the
paper-thin frailty of it as "vista" or position via the
observer. In a black-and-white photo in Del Rio the
infant torn asunder by two disparate figures, one
brown, one white, reaching for both. Descalço. A
warp of jungle, foliage, and innovations. Still
relying on the footpath, bare feet licked by wet
tongues of leaves. Wrapped in cerullean snakes.
Como os olhos contemplam o porto. A carne da
inscrição onde os lábios íntimos tocam. The type of
person who would actually buy a Living Language
course to complete a poem. Must make room for
modem highways.

Cache / Caché?

Cache: the memory hiding place where
frequently-accessed data is kept.

Not as in "net pay" i.e., the web snares but a
net *catches* in its device – you've been around
that roundabout – hyperbole, alliteration of
its "it's a reflex" even if he can't feel a thing,
it comes up just the same. I am privy to what
supermano casts in clipped fray of autumn-
fested fats. (La Parténope, pool, Cabo's sun,
Terri Hatcher's dream vacation.) The
parameters are up in arms over bee pollen,
the portentous pork feast, with its gummy
nutrient blow – montage – découpage –
décolage – triangulation – prognostication –
triage – mestizaje of the Romanesque,
Gothic, and mudéjar – you know there are so
many more directions to which words point
than you admit – Moorish soprano ace racing
past roadside screaming "that history is
POISON", vox populi, smoke, belladonna's
luxurious rouge herbal rush not admiring its
red plumes of fatuous laser aster belled
where we're standing and servitude is its
own conundrum callously craved peeling like
unctuous layers of lava cebolla cropped
inside some egress an acertijo. Voice past
water's short edge faulting practically all
you've had. What kind of data do you hide
and are you coy when you tuck it into the
silky slit of your CPU? Lasting note past
illusory eminence. Orange trees churning a
turn and straight through village's charming
farmhouse with UNIX sign in window. Pasta
chain, daisy boiled, early frost rustles raspy

on newscaster's cue. A section of listless
Mayakofsky rotini between body and
mellifluous brain. Tissue, matter, a system of
coy electrical impulses defines the
undeniable land. For example, remember
riding through the mountain in the back
seat of a car with your leg all in pieces? What
was that? To be certain, you defended the day
before your surgery. (If you were going to die,
you were going to die a Ph.D.) A filet frame
for all those texts you passed through, the
Net as the penultimate site to (Go) Fish.
Meniscus, tendon, rigatone. The adventitious
ligament of not only was his career growing
but he had fallen deeply in love. Ay mamá.

To Achieve Excess, your Vocabulary needs to be at a Level Higher than that of your Competitors

In Wyoming and Southern Erie's
Cattargaus the song stops burning
when languor hits home. Later today
cities responsible for public safety.
Could Scots make costs just to spot
the church steeple area safe again?
The only victim from Western New
payoff is certain to be emotional
even as we crack a crab claw fall
right through this evening's cat's
1 (800) URI-NARY health. There's
no camp on it, it's so well crafted.
Wondering what it was I heard today.
The thousand year old man and the
origin of applause. Hard on the face.
Starving artist quality at rock bottom
starving artist prices (sofa sized
paintings start at only $19.95).
She had answers, real answers.
(Shaking heads in disbelief.) I
take the allergy pill so I can keep
my cat. I can't wait to call again!
Are you concerned or upset because
your husband or lover is having an
affair with your mother? I guess
you're glad to see her! She's about
to reveal to her lost love she's a porn
star. He's complete: he goes from A
to Z and back to A though he can't count.
To every poem its shortcut, to every sand-
wich its Earl. When RAM does not abound
people will always crack your CPU.

Icon Editing

"GUI" – Depending how it's pronounced
it's either Stalin or Gumby

Of course the program is purely writing
stutter your way to visual mnemonics
for example, a trash can represents
a command that no one appreciates
the design of icons is writing too

In icon editing, the absolute Sur-
real lisp that doth accompany
sweeping movements of the mouse –
no cheesy zigzags allowed!

Then also the "vision factor" where
you can't allow yourself to think in boxes –
only to see the large view. Put the squares
together with a fly's compound "I wanna
spy by the sty in my multiple eye"

Ali babest, GUI, choose commands, tart
programs, baba ganoush and skiddle dee
lists of files (eggplant permeates the nodes)
ibn LOOS FILE aka "laundry all over the field"
shark it into the short side of el tilde

tedious and annoying finger sanding
"your name is a poem in itself"
with as many as 4,000 facets
in the case of the home page alone.

"There I Never went Looking
for Extravagant Meanings"

> . . . grappler, sail-maker, block-maker,
> Goods of gutta-percha, papier-maché,
> colors, brushes, brush-making,
> glazier's implements, The veneer and
> glue-pot, the confectioner's ornaments . . .
> WALTER VON WHITMAN

Certain portions cut off by his literal head
from the photos behind. Some fragment of
brass in the transferred file but meant for poem.
Conditions of reading some of those basic
books – or of sending out the work. This
camp "come, ducky, it's time for yum-yum" can
be of some relevance. As if it were in childhood,
your own face staring back but refracted, seen in a
fish eye. Where he ended up fistula. How any photo
could be enlarged. Fission or transfusion. Position
of its constituent parts. "I know it's not me, but
it's too late now, too late to deny – the knowledge"
down to the way the horizontal bar cannot retract
its line without *literally turning into a frog* to leap
frog its way back to the previous post. Its action
"is there, the bits and scraps, flickering on and off,
turn about, winking on the storm, in league to fool me."
There will in fact be a point for 10 point type – near
zeros – so be advised. As it were, no 'soul' in soliloquy
there, no 'mama' in drama, no ham hocks egregious stagnant
cringe wallow sturgeon's last desperate delta despair.
Antonio's old-fashioned and sinecured, "What's shakin'"
lights up the Bexar sky. Pointing to its emendations or
conceptual pontiff to ride behind a Dalkon Shield.
In earlier times, grammar would have had a morally
uplifting influence. Say 'sold' for merchandise and
'Yale' for collagen hopefuls. Calypso collapsing, it fetters
country fresh through pernicious flanks of fetishes. He

can't even admit who is cut off in the photo or why the blast of glare narrowly obscures the remaining figure. Nor why so many clippings, cut guilders, clap half pixels. Is this a gilded image? Too transparent? What leading? As if the window reflects only half the scene inside. How would you explain this? Where does it dovetail? If it's the glass that caused it, then is it the fault of the glazier? All just a matter of trade? That's right, it's simply an occupation.

Balanchine's Words to Printed Passage

While we balance
polyglot of theoretical
mode under pages
are cheaply printed
when come in issue
after issue bound
with staples instead
they hold it is the
issue that print
fades. Replication
alludes. Hand it out
recovers only pen-
umbras of print to
be given away
as A.M. writes that
"underground feeling,
like I'm a Russian
poet in the Stalin era".
Such disregard for
its surface to replicate
within the replica
of text transmitted?
Does not "enter your
system" the way the list
does? Obviously, you
will end up with nothing
but print. Avert the
computer's obsession
with obsessing over
your constant error
straightened corridors
proportion & justifying
what it does. It must
should do best. Take
issue! That is what it

as mimeo modem split
copies of written, drawn,
or typed material form
(obviously a reductive
sense of "text") or imagine
a stencil fitted blue reins
around an inked drum
(originally a trademark)
then to trade such stark
leavings ink stains above
packets and bits driven
mad by spinning nodes
and extra crispy crust
art of the classical pas de
deux list is like people
showing up at your doorstep
the other is a stack of little
magazines to make copious
quite a different story
in terms of irritator.

Scroll

The sea is a scroll but also a typewriter knob
"Yup. 'Found' poems lever this issue wide open."
That's why the button on the right that slides in
its track. The cans didn't lack labels. They were
simply metal translate crack. Of that duo, drop
Verlaine & substitute Percodeine – could always
look into possibilities of scanning them on this
"a series of words preceded by 'my' scrolled two-
words a line down" with contents stamped on
them. It contains the buffer but that is what
writing itself has been. Written or scripted
commodities will never be online – because they
don't cross the line. *Task Netscape (3787) did not
call WSACleanup* connotes a written or
transcripted creation of intellectual property.
The exploitation of these tapes is not a spam!
Writing Rimbaud would have relegated to
antecedent Ethiopian oven. Remember that
México was once an itinerant island and that
Nezahualcóyotl is still referred to as "Señor de
Texcoco" or "Man of Texcoco". We are finally
getting ham radio reports on damage to these
islets. With a Dead Sea Scrolls replica in his desk
drawer. I'll provide details for those interested:
"ip/ipe pin/pine etc, very minimalist; and a very
long list poem" with another verse of seventeen,
in effect starting another. Need some of his
blood titles. People agreed that there is still a
tight web of relationship wherever islanders are.

Gorton's G. & Año Nuevo Laredo

The procedural end of it: take a given day, you do
certain things, then you are exhausted. Friday is
always fish fry day. What is it that takes place
between "the bookends" that you might find a
Servile War, learn that the Spanish highlands
are granite, explore curious fish from Gloucester.
Following Dogtown's rugged, muscular
contractions, garden in Sochi. They claim too
much sand makes it unstable. "Well this isn't
Armenia baby. Buildings don't fall." The
building's marble columns. Where you see the
point of it all, despite fragments lacking fluster
it is all about the strength of pigments. Images,
objects, frames may be reproduced but pigments
exist exclusively in the social. Two pigs named
"The Betrothal" – one a plow, the other a sarong –
"close study of morphological and metamorphic
detail" the other quality of canvas, its hue bleeds
into Gloucester's granite. The old port twist
given away by snow in May. If you weren't a
gypsy, I'd shoot you. The Gorton of it. What does
that have to do with a bell tolling? Shoot, you
saffron addicts! Where Gorky fashioned a good
horse taking to higher elevation. "At a formal
level, the shapes repeat and correspond across
the painting in an almost musical interplay."
How this is a loss of timing and how you might
just wait, husk the colors that swell around you.
Hey, maybe this is what was up that road not
taken! Too much has been placed on New
England and the king's English. What does this
do? – When they herded us up the hill and took
us to the barber shop. "I bet I can make you talk
Indian talk." "How?" – How many times must I
tell you not to fall for those? The <A HREF> to

Man Ray, a multimedia exhibit at the National
Gallery, Washington DC, taking place in
phlegmatic blasts of snow. How I am your
metaphor. *I'll always be figural for you.* Yes, but
will that bring us skin to skin? Despite the
romance someone may just pickpocket your
pocket calculator. You can count on that.
Nothing but happiness – notice its rhythmic
antepenultimate polyrhythmic ramifications?
What others do with life: simply sit there and
hope that by some chance their files and
machines might mesh gears fixed in stele.
Erratic applets eloping to erotic Michoacan.
Feeling threatened by another tongue under
your bell shaped sarong? ¡Que cosa! When you
fire don't think of it as a man but as an argot.
Delirious swans take to deliberate fervor, then
fuck. If you go I go too. Inside white lighthouse
or somewhere you'd imagine it exotic,
dangerous, enervating – say a spiral staircase.
Antipodal oceanographers insist "romantic love
is a packaged projection" thus a pathological
intoxication where you choose the wrong coral
bailiwick. The center of revelry for the past 88
years. That is, no one person is capable of
making you think about them the whole time;
like the bombed ball dropping, it's something
you entrust to yourself. For example, "history".
Before the war, the northern border of México
was at the California-Oregon line. México
included the Southwest (plus a "disputed" strip
from Santa Fe through half of Tejas). At the time
the U.S. govt exaggerated an offense & rode
hootin' into Mexico City, up Chapultepec
(remember the old hymn? "From the halls of

Monte-zooooo-oo-ma") thus taking half of México
for its "eminent" domain. There are a few people
still pissed about this. The point was that after
the parade you would walk the side streets off
Colorado, knee deep in fallen petals, soft and
sweet-sucking as tropical delusional drugs,
picking up discarded fronds. Mountains of
flower parts so libidinous it would take
mechanized organelles to subdue it all: first you
fix them, then you pose a compound question.
"The vanishing apparitions which haunt" Adolfo
Camarillo, his white stallions, and "the inter-
lunations of life" along with Ramón de
Campoamor y Campoosorio's *Doloras* (1845),
Pequeños poemas (1871), and *Humoradas* (new
poetic forms of his invention, 1886), attempting
to bring pottery back into the realm of ideas.
The collecting had enough sweep to include G.,
acclaimed novelist. The point is it takes some
discipline. Clear blocks of time. Make sure you
are sitting, observing, and that food has already
been prepared. Miami's streets the night before,
Pasadena's morning slants next-ward. It's all
there, A to Z in the USA. Azusa's canyons – you
twist up the narrow ravines you would not
believe the high desert land, the back gulleys
where Mexicans picnic in hidden rocky groves,
outcasts from the land that was once all theirs,
the hardened soil, elevated ridges – language
like "as we have seen," "as has been clearly
demonstrated" as a sense of authority, argue
themselves the "elevation" of language of
typologies of of of of discourse. (Or *dis* course
don't run like *dat*. Even on an analog recorder.)
Watch who you accuse of an ideological bent.

For example, if you're going to say Guillén's perspective is engagé or militant, then you should admit the Lord's Prayer and the Monroe Doctrine are equally as combative. Cobalt, San Bernadino copse-speckled ravines, its parched peccadillo, armadillo fantasies of just marching east and east into the final dawn of surf suffocation. This also recalls a popular locution for "this is my freakin' mountain". That is when you want to bring in a preponderance of supplementary material, just whack 'em with your AACR2. In the highest areas there is a spring where you can fill bottles to bolster, booty further, or explore counter argument. Incandescent synecdoche topless on the ledge and light-haired children frolic in sumptuous orange beams of sun. Is there no other place you could ever be? Note that this is an arid, rocky stretch of peaks hidden in steepness from the vocabulary. A lexicon that by nature has no boundary by type of language. Not only a difference in style but a preponderant question of whether "person" is allowed in this writing, whether initiating such forms of life is, of itself, an end, or the last island enclave of suburban homes. Arid, rocky stretch of peaks hidden in steepness from the panopticon, or simply made to cower in the beaten, littered woods. Never for once forgetting the cars passing overhead, your edgeless glossary, or canyon warning signs, "azusa" being "skunk" in indigenous languages.

The Reed Heads

the white centrist
petted a python &
brought it into her house
to make inferences

Only give the text passages, the quotes, not even show and tell.
Just completed an argument & now we have this whiz bang stuff.
I'm just using a screen instead of an easel to do what we've
been doing for hundreds of years. Ever finger-paint? If that's the
Mac metaphor then the PC version is like painting with chopsticks –
and someone else got all the prawns! He wants to use a novel.
He was sight-reading bar codes. Politics is a giant video game
for billionaires. The worst friar attack in recent memory. These
fibers have never been described in literature. Here is a link
that everyone's been looking for, between the brain and heavy
metal. He severs unknown tissues to engorge cerebral access.
Graphics show pieces of the puzzle. May advance theories
based on that evidence. How do you sculpt angels? "I take
a piece of marble and I remove everything that is *not* an angel."
It's the not there that is there. "Everything having to do with
human affairs is open to some possible or imaginary doubt."
She was at the mirage. Hoping to argue why the cameras
should be turned on. Instead of the jagged noise you actually
saw two defensive woods. Bad words to the back of her head.
That final coup de grace had smooth margins. To see if there is
premeditation and deliberation. For your palms to be cut your
hands have to be open. They found a will – and some photographs
which she put in her safe deposit box. That little pill relieves for
nine hours. The stars are fighting back, trying to reclaim their
image and their dignity. Post-homicidal conduct asks no questions.
Says she proselytizes for money. That maybe you can spend the rest
of your life with her. What life is all about? The call of the road
not the road itself. The glacial standards of this case, not its polarity.
Its citizen time-line witnesses our journey towards the City of Justice.
This is the fish hook cut. Theater is part of the facts in this tense.
Some real problems in their leaps. Wrapping himself in the flag.

Garbage-in garbage-out theory of scientific evidence. The sentence
that starts "If you can't recall the station names" should have a comma
there instead of a period. Drum a catch phrase into the posse. Twins
of deception that bring you a message you cannot trust. Hold a mirror
up to the faces of North America. Got a question for the askew angel
of time? We are not alone on this shell, we are sharing the sea. Science
is no better than the horse it rode in on. The people who constitute its
chain of custody system. Performance over substance. Substance versus
style. An escalation of emotion. Look at risk factors. Divorcees looking
for a good hate fuck in a bar. Will the Congressman be in Betty Ford
more than Gerald Ford? When was the last time you really had fun
in a car? Would you consider sex to be a social contact? Are you
single and available today? Hearing is better than speaking.
A penny solved. Writing is to him what flesh is to us all.

"Wits Have Short Memories & Dunces None"

This is the final act of computation, the first time I take it – that
as a matter of case. Foxglove motherboard – larger slots plot
stickers "The first time I have seen 'duende' translated as goblin.
That is a little alarming, given that a popular brand of toilet
paper in Mexico is *Duende*." Morgan's morning hunched into
Popocatépetl hood; its illusive backdrop & smiles road's handy
abyss. The hole in my Volkswagen's engine plugged with a
pencil so that, before the engine blew, the car would always
blow its pencil. For long trips, I simply kept a box of new pencils
in my glove box. This always impressed my dates, though for a
writer it just made sense. Lunar landscale. Prepared to desert
there. Across its radial can. Vestibule removed – cactus played
anonymous Mayapán stain. In vest in harachis. In a volcano its
Taxco shelter implode.
> The loss of a formal "you" may seem a small thing to native
> English speakers. In the United States, the language had lost
> its thee's and thou's by the time of the American Revolution.
> But in Europe these forms survived for centuries and with-
> stood many of the changes of the modern age.
Inserts some HTML or HTML+ cookie. The point is then placed
where you want to type in the information for that cookie. If you
call the command with a prefix argument (typing C-u latah), the
cookie chocolate-chips the current region. Bit-shot pin-stripes
with byte-time impact. A record? We can alternate its onLoad
event and two-dimensional array with live-or-die clichés.
Installing a modified version of the HTTPD daemon (web server).
Several people have observed the conglomeration of commercial
presses and their retreat from poets as loss-leaders. Web writing
is writing in that, what you write must be readable from the
perspectives of completely different browsers. Really not unlike
the academic paper or a packet of coupons delivered to every
home. Metamail: incomplete multi-part message. Unexpected
confusion about the music of the poem? We'll send you new
information about hearing loss and a free coupon.

The Lettrist

FOR PUBLIC INTEREST, CONVENIENCE & NECESSITY
people vote for which commercial they like best,
parole, parabola, anesthetic, what longitude, what
largesse, peaches, penumbras, what boys running
through the watermelons – what steaks and
whiskey are promised to unite them against the
long speculation of who would threaten what has
become the hallmark of democracy: the choice of
software, what brand name, its knobs. Not many
would admit how significant this has become.
Think of the Caicos, Turks, and felaheens, the
Abacos and Frazier's Hog Cay, and the exciting
thing – how such a degree of choice has influenced
the future of writing itself! Who knows what effect
an author's acceptance of Word's default settings
will have on future humanistic analyses of their
work! What corruption! What hidden files! These
are not mere choices in product but more akin to
the choice of spouse, running mate, or place of
habitation. Your entire spectrum of creative habit is
affected. That is, one program may make it more
convenient to cut and paste, another to run macros.
Not to mention later intrusions like automatic word
completion! Or compulsive automasturbation, spell
chuck, erectile dysfunction keys. What folly, what
frivolity, what a capricious sprite fingering the
pudendal cleavage of your over-lubricated cleft
motherboard! What's at stake here is that we *do*
follow the dictates of a given machine. How are our
decisions a response to our choice of machine? The
spouse we choose says something about us too,
don't it? Along what silicon Champs-Elysées does
our machine torque the choice our writing will
take? What peonies, what ablutions, and what
adumbrations. What numb knuckles pummeling

the prostate. What about literal physical size? Think of this. Some day one will hear: the traveling writer's texts became more scrunched before the turn of the millennium and why? Because laptops were designed *not to fit laps* – but to fit airplane fold-down tray tables, the most economic width for suspending in-transit human form! The story has everything: curvaceous women, headlines, & lawsuits where this country dips its sartorial nose into the busty tropes of our erogenous zones. What could possibly be wrong with your half or hard-cocked finances? It only makes sense to pay $240,000 for an $80,000 house over 30 years. People with money *do* have a right to more money, don't they? This never changes? Since it takes money to get elected, those elected have a vested interest in protecting the interests of money. Could that be an appurtenant factor? And some say the only answer is communism! Well, if the system works, no need to change it! Would you be so kind as to define 'irony' for me? You'd have to rent reality bites. (Does the title of that film mean 'reality nibbles' – or 'computer slices of reality' – or is it just trying to say 'reality sucks'?) Is there a tie-in between this and the German high Romantic resource, Goethe bytes? Do we rush to more conclusions? What was the point in carving those huge icons up there – and how did they decide just who would make the cliff? Was it so obvious at the time? Say you wanted images to represent, respectively, the nation's founding, philosophy, unity, & expansion. Well of course it'd take 12 years using pneumatic drills and dynamite, it would be obvious. Who would we dynamite? How about native peoples? Or maybe we could announce trumped up charges and invade any country with oil. Perhaps we could even allow thousands of years of human history to be trashed in the process *and* bag dad's shortfall. Anyone want disenfranchised with their burger? It was John Gutzon de la Mothe Borglum's friendship with Rodin that led him to concentrate on overstatement and Hitchcock's lugubrious mordant swank that threw it off the ledge. Apparently, a lot depended on the analytical quality of the voice. Beside the white chickadees was a southerner on the 'pone. Because of its inflections, the accent was unintelligible. Within seconds, the crackerjack interpreter adjusted. It was like bayoneting a reb in a Civil War of prosodies. Not civil but prosaic. Oh Prosac! Or the sperm sac. No yolk – it's economics that count. Behold the tweed-clad intellectuals chatting up the cappuccino diva at old dormer square. First reason given was that she is too old for it. The second, that they don't have time. Meanwhile, since that particular book was not available in San Antonio, one enterprising man "went up somewhere in Texas" and did manage to find it. Its stories, that must-not-die point of view; see, it's a whole new cannibalism doing the diss'n on a laptop versus the age-old labors of scribes. Don't get too analytical. It's simply that the methods have changed. Once what card sets, markers in library wooden benches, the touch of leather spines told, can now be neatly P-slipped on a PDA. Hey you don't wanna attach meaning to those old land sine curves slingin' manhattoes round the silver blind of Soho, do you? Or the ol' git trying to park genteel-like in drifts of metonymy? G'wan! Can you read it in the Twelfth century? The Bills were long shots even then. As in, the true birth date of the King, the Holy See, SAWPro's 32 bit architecture,

Lord knows it changes every century. Do you like
the price of your surge protector? Lonely? DATA loss
could be worse. And we all know, it's hard to find a
good Marxist bride in Williamsville. It ain't the font
that's doin' it but the percentile of zaum. "Lekhnu,"
"to write" or to conjugate, to scribe, or paw.
Namaste, chitthi lekhdaihunuhunchha? Hoina, ma
nepali padhdaichhu. Can you sound it out? Auraten
aur larkian. Mard aur larke. Kitaben aur akhbar.
Hotal men kamre. Score. Wherever his master is,
there his dog will be also. "De la caña sale azúcar,
azúcar para el café." Xalapa, Coyoacán, Colima,
Lagunas Carrizalillo & La María. Jo chahe ho. – Kya
hua? – Sup? – Please give me a return ticket to
Churchgate. Moi shepaw. O choptaw. Uprosodista!
Slike agrant uppaginst de reetham un den ein work
gehat. Yaba daba doo all ova yoo sho. Or is that
Elizabeth Shue? Aur eck bin ein tar und La Brea'd
uppaginst de boulevard angelinoed in the angel
ranked skank. All I'm askin for is an angle! Knots o
knobs o Kulu Manaali's streak point blanc. You can
always work off a pound of fat, but you can never
work off a coma. A sound card that neither makes a
sound nor was a sound investment. Mimeo type,
yellowing Cuban paper, hand-painted covers of
Oaxacan offset presses with their pastels and
vibrant rose. People pink, perchance hyperbola, vote
anesthetic, in shameless semidarkness, comic
geometry. Conic section of laconic clone, olive tree,
anchovy pear, pitanga, uniflora, its ellipse, its oval.
Psidium littorale, a curve generated by the
intersection of a plane and a circular icon.
Persimmons, Royaumont's armaniac, the painted
chapels of Michoacán. Purple strawberry guava in a
commonplace book. Relaxation in shavasana. A

language that's all verb, see. Say, Cindy Crawford in
a backless toadflax see-through. Surgically
enhanced angels snake trophy wives. Or so the
coffee flower's brown writing eyes low. Ô slow
chapeau, radio, comme il faut. Bummalo or Bombay
duck. Ruck slat. Where it's at. Its full-length
hunched over iced DAT caveat. Verbs that you keep
in a manila envelope and guard assiduously, in
flagrante delicto. Carpe deum or café conjunto.
Televidentes, oyentes. "That's right, you're not from
Texas." For example, accents may not indicate
sound at all, nor may they necessarily indicate
stress. The point is they might define a new word
entirely, as if "si" were the same as "sí"! Do you see?
We use a gerund, generalize "is refreshing" since
our latitude seldom allows inanimate objects to
perform their actions on us! I.e., el refresco de
naranja me refrescó bastante. We make it all
passive! ¡Que horror! A Saturday morning with
conjunto music low. Do you hear, oyentes? C'mon
you hairy backed Marys, let's choose sides. If I'm
captain, who's Tenile? Quepo, cabe, cabo, Quechua.
Linear regression's significant obsession. Own one
and you'll understand. Where you plunder, I
innovate. La bufanda (booooof – it blows, see?),
scarf, balanza, scale or to be aburrrrrrrrido, borrred
by etymology, a burlesque in JavaScript. "I'm calling
to retrieve you from the subjunctive." On that note,
what a difference in register between "Haz lo que
quieres" ("Do what you want") and "Haz lo que
quieras" ("Do what you will"). Or objects with
gender. "Para" vs. "por". ¡Mayombe – bombe –
mayombé! Usualmente i.e., ooswalmentay. A
nanoverb squeaks a squall as you call. A medium
crash, a squawk, a rock crash, a splash. A ping ride,

[94]

a medium thin crash, China boy low, tin vacuole.
Halls, rooms, plates, un tenedor, un cuchillo, una
cuchara – it's glorious, one for each of us in the
chorus. Cucaracha flange delay rotary speaker.
Multieffects, versatile "adjust" knob as the word
said. Morphemes made me what I am today, a
spicier condenser of radio static. Together we
celebrate wickedly low sodium. Refund: me ma ny
vt ct. Dopo il Porfiriato. The old question, were you a
Villista or Zapatista, a Carrancista or Obregonista –
not a heuristic Huerista! Obedezco pero no cumplo.
Celaya, Jonacatepec, and the Plan of Agua Prieta.
Umberto Eco? Shhhh, écoutez! Wanna blukambalo?
Whee si ankee! Mat awful wataneeyou kadim o il
hadith. Hi dee kloom verkleidet bikini ist. Schöne,
schöne, under the moone. Tais toi. Ta gueule! Jeudi
j'ai dit maudit mots. Nasi goreng. Bami goreng. Ben
de iyiyim, tesekkür ederim. Güle güle. Merhaba,
seni seviyorum! Bendy eel yew yam, tea shaker
arider rim. Ghouly ghouly. Mayor have a semi-CV,
you rum. Whee see yeh tapiwano song. Yanka yanka
toma hanka. Me lissa toe may. Baba stry san zing zo
dull. What me scurry? It's my metrical line.
Wherever his master is, there his dog will be also.
Main chakta hun hindi bolna. Pate aur tar. Pate aur
pits. La Brea's famous pâté de tar pits. Jo chahe ho.
Let it rock aur let it scroll. Which more clearly
transcribed might come out all in symbols (like
marking expletives in comics) – though I wouldn't
want you to presume there's any similar level of
excess here.

NOTES

There is the sense in these poems that no language boundary is imperme-
able. Thus, languages mix, form part of the process of making poetry,
whether Spanish, other non-English languages, or the codes and proto-
cols of digital writing.

Of note is the relation some of these poems share with digital poetry.
Many of these texts have had digital versions, have grown, have been
"sounded", or have been co-developed within the digital medium. Thus the
print version, an avatar of the digital process that shaped it, could not exist
without the digital experimentation that gave it voice. It is the author's
thesis that every instance of a poem is in some sense a variant, one possi-
bility among many; digital poetry explores the interactivity of these vari-
ants. Within such a sound eco-system, the poem samples the richness of
texts co-existing in a landscape of larger poetic sustenance.

Many of these poems have also profited by the possibilities that digital
technology offers to the creative process through forms of digital experi-
mentation such as algorithmic generation, Web searches, Unix processes
(such as greps), computer errors, early hypertextual mechanisms, and
other textual production methods. This is not to say that the texts were not
composed. Rather, that digital processes provided stimulation, compan-
ionship, succor, alma, and a more various range of choices to draw from
in the construction of these poetry objects.

Some of the digital versions of these poems, as well as other selected
digital and text projects are available at the Electronic Poetry Center
Glazier author page (http://epc.buffalo.edu/authors/glazier).

Following are some brief notes about these landscapes of digital activity.

The Parts

A number of the poems in *The Parts* originally appeared in *RIF/T* and on
  the LINEbreak program. *RIF/T* was an influential electronic magazine
  that predating the Web in its origins and published until early in the
  Web environment. LINEbreak was the first Internet literary audio
  programming project. In these poems, I was motivated by the new
  possibilities of the medium, driven by the difficulties of casting words
  in the pre-Web digital environment, excited by their transmissibility,
  and influenced by the vocabulary of early technology: mark-up conven-
  tions, network protocols, and computer code – themselves ways of work-
  ing *with words.*

"Five Pieces for Sound File", following the proclamation in the opening
  epigraph by Kerouac, existed first as a sound file experiment, published
  in a CD-ROM issue of *The Little Magazine.* Initially, there was little atten-
  tion to text, this poem growing from experiments with the visual
  appearance of its sounds using an audio editing program of the time.

"PARSINGS – from *E*" is an abstract of a large early hypertext verbal network written for the Web.

"The Parts" itself was inspired, in part, by the first Internet video and by the Internet graphics that predated the Web. In those days, the user would have to download a set of files via anonymous FTP, assemble them, then run them through a decoding program to render the image. The packet architecture of the Web and the way that a computer stores information, not conterminously, but scattered throughout the hard drive, led to the postulation that digital writing (and indeed all writing), rather than being a whole (the common illusion), is a specific conglomeration of *parts* of writings.

Semilla De Calabaza (Pumpkin Seed)

This section is a voyage into the possibilities of a linguistic America that is larger than the U.S.'s presence as dominant entity. Indeed, American languages are diverse and widely-distributed; they only need be sounded to be seen. The section also has to do with hispanismo as it exists in both the first and third worlds in the face of a totalizing Anglo culture, history, and ethos. Digital writing was one means to explore how language and languages can both be there and also can not, and how other forms of writing, such as the visual and the aural, can inform this larger landscape of language.

"White-Faced Bromeliads on 20 Hectares", the opening sequence in the section is an "iteration" of a digital poem. It offers an impulse-chance assembled confluence of data elements from its digital watershed, the fully-developed digital poem. In its online version, "Bromeliads" contains two possibilities for each line of the poem. It uses JavaScript to generate poem versions whose textual dynamic is one dramatized by the possibilities of subtle variability. Every ten seconds, the online version of the poem is reconfigured, drawing from an alternate for one or more of each displayed line. While a randomizing algorithm determines whether variants are or are not selected for display, construction of the architecture of possibilities is according to author design. "Bromeliads" is meant to explore subtle changes and unpredictability. Even with only two possibilities for each line, the potential for such a dynamic poem is striking: each 8-line poem in "Bromeliads" offers 512 possible versions, making two identical readings of the sequence nearly impossible. The fully functional digital version of this work is available on the Web. (See the URL given on the opening page to this book.)

"Bromeliads" originated in a trip I made to the town of La Fortuna in northwestern Costa Rica. All the neighboring towns had been eradicated by a recent eruption of the Volcán Arenal but this one town had

[98]

been spared. (It was renamed "Good Luck" as a consequence.) As I lay awake during nights illuminated by the sputterings and animated by the rumblings of the active volcano, I got to thinking about variability, and this application of JavaScript came into my head. The digital version of the poem came directly from my notes, with the print version later informed by the insights that resulted from observing the unpredictable radical juxtapositions the code produced.

In "La Habana / Mar" the sections "On Your Marx," and "In Che's A Way", and "Viva Zapata" all have digital versions that are strikingly different. The digital manifestations of these poems included computer animation and are visual, colorful and aural. These digital versions provided a cinematographic view of the textual material, providing keen insight into how the text could later exist on the page, i.e., not just in print but *en vivo*. (See the URL given on the opening page to this book.)

As to the pumpkin seed in the title of this section, one time I was on a 14-hour journey in Costa Rica, crossing a mountain range in a dilapidated bus with bad shocks, enduring hour after hour of hairpin turns. A gaggle of North Americans on the bus complained vociferously about the inadequacy of the country and its transportation system. At one point, we stopped and boys came on the bus to sell home-baked pumpkin muffins. I began eating mine and found a pumpkin seed in the middle of it, another imperfection. I let the seed linger in my mouth thinking, this is the gift of language I have been given: to have this vocabulary on my tongue, to simply participate in other ways of being in the world. The section explores multiple ways of being in that linguistic and material world.

Leaving Loss Glazier

The poems in this sequence exhibit the discovery process of writing is to write in the expanded scenes of textuality Web-writing provides. These poems chronicle the early days of the Web and the rise of panoptic software and manipulative word processing programs. At a certain point, the social possibilities of digital writing turned a corner. We entered the now-common domination of totalitarian big-corporation operating systems. The reality became an illusion akin to the Las Vegas strip, predominantly glitter with little depth. In the spirit of the film, "Leaving Las Vegas" the new operating system of the time, Windows 95 (the harbinger of "ca-chings" to come), was the perfect venue for a showdown, an ideal city for the final stanzas that obliterate the self.

Playing on the theme of self in a much different sense, the poems in this section more importantly explore the loss of self as it occurs in the increasingly present paradigm of distributed poetics, including the poetics of radical disjunction, of variability, and of a more heterogeneous "American" language. A sense of distributed poetics is of keen relevance to this day. ¡Oye!

Printed in the United States
149192LV00001B/13/A

9 781844 710010